EPISTLES

Also by Mark Jarman

To the Green Man (2004)

Body and Soul: Essays on Poetry (2002)

The Secret of Poetry (2001)

Unholy Sonnets (2000)

Questions for Ecclesiastes (1997)

Rebel Angels: 25 Poets of the New Formalism,
coedited with David Mason (1996)

The Reaper Essays coedited with Robert McDowell (1996)

Iris (1992)

The Black Riviera (1990)

Far and Away by Mark Jarman (1985)

The Rote Walker (1981)

North Sea (1978)

Epistles

poems
Mark Jarman

Sarabande  Books
LOUISVILLE, KENTUCKY

No part of this book may be reproduced without written permission of the publisher. Please direct inquiries to:

Managing Editor
Sarabande Books, Inc.
2234 Dundee Road, Suite 200
Louisville, KY 40205

Library of Congress Cataloging-in-Publication Data

Jarman, Mark.
    Epistles : poems / by Mark Jarman. — 1st ed.
        p.   cm.
    ISBN 978-1-932511-52-9 (hardcover : alk. paper) — ISBN 978-1-932511-53-6 (pbk. : alk. paper)
    1. Spirituality—Poetry. 2. Religious poetry, American. I. Title.
    PS3560.A537E75 2007
    811'.54—dc22   2006037520

ISBN-13 (cloth): 978-1-932511-52-9
ISBN-13 (paper): 978-1-932511-53-6

Cover image: *Study of Clouds*, by John Constable. Oil on paper (laid down on canvas). Provided courtesy of The Whitworth Art Gallery, The University of Manchester.

Manufactured in Canada
This book is printed on acid-free paper.

Sarabande Books is a nonprofit literary organization.

This project is supported in part by an award from the National Endowment for the Arts.

The Kentucky Arts Council, a state agency in the Commerce Cabinet, provides operational support funding for Sarabande Books with state tax dollars and federal funding from the National Endowment for the Arts, which believes that a great nation deserves great art.

For Terri Witek

Table of Contents

IV

V

VI

Acknowledgments

American Poetry Review: Epistles 2, 6, 7, 10, 11, 14, 17, 23, 24, and 26

The Atlanta Review: Epistle 20

Barrow Street: Epistles 8, 9, and 15

Crazyhorse: Epistle 1

Denver Quarterly: Epistle 29

Five Points: Epistles 13, 18, 19, and 27

The Hudson Review: Epistles 16 and 21

Image: Epistles 22 and 25

Meridian: Epistles 3, 4, and 5

Michigan Quarterly Review: Epistle 28

Seneca Review: Epistle 12

The Yale Review: Epistle 30

Epistle 4 ("We want the operation") appeared in *The Best American Poetry 2000* (Scribners). Epistle 14 ("When the thief comes") appeared in *Great American Prose Poems: From Poe to the Present* (Scribners).

I want to thank Michelle Boisseau, Christopher Buckley, Kate Daniels, Andrew Hudgins, Marie Kaczorek, and Terri Witek for reading this book in early drafts and doing what they could to help me make it better.

Now faith is the substance of things hoped for, the evidence of things not seen.

Hebrews 11: 1

It must be I want life to go on living.

Robert Frost

EPISTLES

One

1. If I were Paul

Consider how you were made.

Consider the loving geometry that sketched your bones, the passionate symmetry that sewed flesh to your skeleton, and the cloudy zenith whence your soul descended in shimmering rivulets across pure granite to pour as a single braided stream into the skull's cup.

Consider the first time you conceived of justice, engendered mercy, brought parity into being, coaxed liberty like a marten from its den to uncoil its limber spine in a sunny clearing, how you understood the inheritance of first principles, the legacy of noble thought, and built a city like a forest in the forest, and erected temples like thunderheads.

Consider, as if it were penicillin or the speed of light, the discovery of another's hands, his oval field of vision, her muscular back and hips, his nerve-jarred neck and shoulders, her bleeding gums and dry elbows and knees, his baldness and cauterized skin cancers, her lucid and forgiving gaze, his healing touch, her mind like a prairie. Consider the first knowledge of otherness. How it felt.

Consider what you were meant to be in the egg, in your parents' arms, under a sky full of stars.

Now imagine what I have to say when I learn of your enterprising viciousness, the discipline with which one of you turns another into a robot or a parasite or a maniac or a body strapped to a chair. Imagine what I have to say.

Do the impossible. Restore life to those you have killed, wholeness to those you have maimed, goodness to what you have poisoned, trust to those you have betrayed.

Bless each other with the heart and soul, the hand and eye, the head and foot, the lips, tongue, and teeth, the inner ear and the outer ear, the flesh and spirit, the brain and bowels, the blood and lymph, the heel and toe, the muscle and bone, the waist and hips, the chest and shoulders, the whole body, clothed and naked, young and old, aging and growing up.

I send you this not knowing if you will receive it, or if having received it, you will read it, or if having read it, you will know that it contains my blessing.

2. Listening to you

Listening to the call-in show yesterday, I knew that you were not happy. You asked about weight loss. You asked about aphrodisiacs. You asked about your children and their contempt for your way of life. You asked about travel to other worlds.

I drove to my next appointment, and as I listened to each of your voices, with its muffled desire, I wanted to stop at the nearest phone and call in a response.

Money would make you happy. Sex would make you happy. Power. Leisure. You are denied them. Why live? Something makes you wish to keep living. Some money. Some sex. Power. Leisure.

Is the dollar unhappy it is not a ten? Yes, you would say, the soiled soft dollar bill with its short life is not happy. But the cent endures, the nickel and dime, the quarter, turning green, black.

Go to the burnt out bulb to study the beauty of failure. There in its violated space, the arms raised but the filaments incinerated, the flashmark like the feathery white face of a moth, it is now cool and detached, the ruined throne room of a dead sun king.

What is like you in dissatisfaction? Trees that grow hunchbacked in the search for light. Water bleeding everywhere it can. Bacteria awakening in decay. The urge to breed by division.

Satisfaction is death.

Sit at your kitchen table with the phone in your hand, the radio on as you listen to others penetrate the house of fame, their voices entering the cloud of the elect, shedding anonymity like a sunburn, and consider that the energy speaking from your radio which will connect you with the universe is already shaped as you.

Your body passes through matter, in a shape moving through time. Thus a wave begins in water, passes a life in air, breaks, and enters the earth, or enters fire, then earth. Always in motion, appearing to be one with its body, but always leaving it behind. What you call yourself, these hands, this torso and buttocks, folded legs and damp feet, is no more than the light that lets you see it.

Think of yourselves as planets, cities, forts, hives, ideal communities, rain forests, oases. But it will also work to be a kidney, a dumpster, a horse pat, cud, a colony of germs, a night school.

If I could stop and make a phone call with this message, I would. Instead I will stop at the next church office with my communion ware, robes and stoles, Sunday school lessons, holiday decorations. I know what the pastors in the poor churches who give me ten minutes of their time are offering. The middleaged man they see, opening his sample cases, displaying a new book of Advent meditations for youngsters, is not all that I am. I believe that, even though it is hidden from me.

3. On the island of the pure in heart

On the island of the pure in heart, we did not see God. But an influx of pink scallop shells, each the size of a fingertip, covered the sand.

On the island of the meek, a stench drove us back to the ship.

On the island of the poor in spirit, a glassy blankness came down like rain and asked a riddle that stumped us.

Riflemen among spraypainted rocks fired at us, on the island of the righteous. One rock said, "Byron, 18—."

On the island of the merciful, we obtained mercy.

On the island of the peacemakers, we depleted our numbers by hand-to-hand combat, until there were only two of us—a soul and a body.

Even as they urged us to depart, on the island of the persecuted, they begged us to stay.

4. We want the operation

We want the operation because we want the cure.

We are naked and open unto his eyes, though draped in sterile cloth. He is quick and powerful, piercing even to the dividing of soul and spirit, though both choose amnesia. He separates them, even as he divides the joints and marrow, discerning the thoughts and intents of the heart in a small, vestigial, rooted, and determined thing.

Later, he shows how the sick part was woven in, by lacing the middle finger of his right hand, his knife hand, among the fingers of his left. He found it, severed it, stitched closed the wound it left, then backed out of the larger wound, shutting each layer behind him. An eye tips each of his bloody fingers.

There was that instant when the anesthetic took hold, and some triviality—the chrome rim of a lamp—slipped from focus. Our eyes clung to the slippery shine. Then, they forgot even the darkness they entered.

So the cut came, the skin parted, the fat, the muscle, the sheaths of membrane, the different colored layers, all doused in bright oxygenated blood, which was expertly sprayed away, so the invasion would be clear.

But first the skin was shaved, then painted with antiseptic, the tomb jewel color of ochre. First the diagnosis was made. First the protocol and the procedure were recommended. We wanted the operation because we wanted the cure.

First the morning that we woke with a new unease that did not fade by lunchtime. First the night we could not sleep, as sleep kept cracking underfoot. First the hand of a companion, asking, "Are you all right?" First our own voice answering, saying, "I don't know." And the voice that stated frankly, "No, you're not."

Thus God performs his surgery, closing and opening simultaneously, always with new reasons to go in.

5. My travels in Abyssinia

My travels in Abyssinia are at an end. I hear three kinds of singing around me at this instant. Each voice (it is night) is pleading. I need a *Dictionary of Commerce and Navigation*. I need silk stockings woven with elastic threads. I need cartridges, fruit pastilles. I need your word. Your solemn touch. A simple answer.

You know what it is like to cease to exist to everyone but yourself. The cyclone that damaged the national art treasure made you homeless. On the day of the spectacular assassination, you discovered the first symptom of your final illness. Indeed, you know what it is like to exist *like* everyone else. And yet you live, your name is official, you can point to the place that says you are who you say you are.

I can see you in a drained tide pool, a grainy lump that closes on the delicate tentacles of the sea anemone. What you wouldn't give to taste the salty mineral soup in which you flower. But the entire ocean has turned its profound interest elsewhere. And whole species die, not to mention those, like you, who thought they were one of a kind.

We are engendered by the same obscurity. And we can imagine that it loves us, as the irrational number loves the infinite places to the right of its decimal point. Buried in the deepest reaches of 22 divided by 7, beyond which lie enormous wastes of energy and perseverance, we can see necessity. The previous number gives birth to the next. That is the reason we live. Let this knowledge cradle you. The lullaby that rocks your heart says you will not be, only because you are.

Now as so often before, I have given when I hoped to receive. I need a manual on irrigation technique. I need tincture of benzoin to harden the blisters on my heels. I need a token of your esteem. Before I board the ferry, I want to see a courier pressing through the crowd, who will reach me as I put my foot on the bow and hand me... But how can you respond as I would have you respond?

You know how it is to set out, laden with all you will leave enroute. To look back and see the years, like chairs and tables, abandoned in the desert. To see days going under like trunks of china in the horse latitudes. Weeks and months jettisoned and floating in the zero gravity of space. You know how it is to take stock by repeating *at least, at least,* until all you have is your life.

Let this be like the prayer that God will always answer. The one that gives thanks for everything and asks for nothing.

Two

6. I have lost my explanation

I have lost my explanation for the divine plan.

The vehicle for my metaphor was either the depths of π or it was the trajectory of DNA. I think something about the existence of numbers going on infinitely backwards reassured me. But how from that do I extrapolate love?

Mathematics calls across distances. The angels are sines and cosines. And so on. But can heaven choose between one and many? There is no warmth in knowing God's guts are a string of irrational numbers.

And I know that the very way we die, that is, the way we grow old and die, is buried in us. Even in the child who dies, the old woman or man is buried, never to be born, but waiting. And I think that shows—but I can't unpick the knot there, either.

I don't want to explain it all in terms of the family again. How the parents create and love their creation, and that is Godlike. And how the children disappoint them, and that is human, and the parents punish, and that is Godlike. Or how the parents withdraw, also Godlike, and the children leave and make their own lives and their parents recede in daily importance, in any importance. Or how the parents die, shattering their children, who begin to think they were made by an absence. Or the parents divorce, belying their love, and shame permeates their creation like an element of the air, the oxygen that lights a match and lets us breathe. As its nucleus explodes, as it must eventually explode, and its particles carom and conjoin, a family's breakdown imitates a random plan and not the one that I am trying to remember how to explain.

I have lost my explanation.

But I know of someone who has proved the universe is digital, programmed by some divine hand and a mind which, like a rain forest, is burning. Our interface is smoke, shaped and lit to look like fingers of a glove, columns of a flooded city, eroded buttes, pipe organs, something we know. And because of that—our knowing—something we do not know.

7. *There is no formula*

There is no formula for bliss, yet why not pretend there is? Begin with
the sour cloud that comes with failure, the aftermath that lingers, a
chemical scent impossible to mask. There are surviving children to
entertain. They have devised something cheerful to do, without toys, on
a cement plaza. Watching them the gloom shifts to one side. That
distraction is bliss.

Or think of it as the saliva smeared on each suction cup of a bird feeder
stuck to a study window. Fill the feeder with seed, and the cardinal pairs,
which the children have named—the High Hats with red crests and the
Baldies with black leather skullcaps—make a metallic chirp. Blinds
down, hear it. The formula for bliss makes music on the window glass.

Formula, little form, principle, equation, successful convention,
repeated successfully. Inside the body, happiness tells its good news to
every cell. So many small epiphanies in a promised land. Formulas for
bliss include: good weather, absorbing work, anticipation of sex,
lightness of being. Careful, though; don't float away.

Here's one: a mackerel sky splits into mares' tails. Morning traffic lines up, pauses, as if enthralled, and a song comes on the radio that holds an entire past summer like a bubble on its lips. Later, October shadows lie across the burnished streets like bars of elegiac music, immortal, even as they fade.

It should be some sequence anyone can follow. For example, the mountain that is little more than a hillock may be climbed in an hour. A sunny cowpath goes to the top. There the entire valley opens— limestone cliffs and vineyards, village roofs and the church spire—like the meaning of a parable. The clouds above provide a mood, minor in the majority of the sky. On the summit, everywhere, a new flower appears whose name is in the book you've brought along.

And here, because you know what I am telling you, bliss is the state of someone else who loves how you taste, the scent of someone else, remaining with you like a skin of phosphorescence, lighting the daywarmed, moonless asphalt road followed into sleep.

All of this sounds so easy.

Explain bliss as music, to someone who can't hear it. Explain it as sex, to someone who can't feel it. Explain it as spectacle, to someone who can't see it. Explain it as the aroma of mother's milk, to someone who can't smell it. Explain it as the salt sweetness of a lover's skin, to someone who can't taste it.

In fact, explain this state of grace to the graceless, the unloved and the unlovable. Explain it to the nuisance whining for attention, who will, as always, ruin it for everyone. Unloved, he will discover that to be loved is to be dissolved. Hated, she will learn that to be forgiven is to be erased. Overwhelmed, as her feet kick out and his head knocks back, as the wave lifts, hurls, holds them under, and repeats, they will find that the air they breathed held the secret.

Verbum caro factum est. The word is made flesh. That is bliss. But for those to whom the body is pain, to themselves and others, bliss comes when flesh is made into words. Say, "Now you are released." Say, "Now you are pure spirit." Say, "Now all the pleasure you have been denied is turned into poetry." Say, "God has committed you to memory."

8. Each of us at the community service center

Each of us at the community service center is waiting to be released. One soul, one body, we are waiting to divide, to enter the glory of our separate selves. We will take off the uniform of light, with the stitchery that names us each with the same name, and put on darkness again, our own, bagged and stowed when we entered, so long ago.

Here time is like a sense blocked by nerve damage. When we leave, we will again taste the way seconds dissolve. Touch the electric skin of minutes. Hear the hour chime. Smell glad day, glum day, every day. And looking ahead to their vanishing point, we will see the years.

In the community service center, razor wire, TV, the smoke of cigarettes joined in a single hovering body—these unite us. We have learned to love one another as ourselves. We have learned cookery, cosmetology, creative writing, and accounting.

We have one story, and each of us has polished a single facet. We will take the story and hammer it into bits, retrieving the particle that belongs to us. We will break up the team, sell off the lots. For it is the living and breathing part torn from the whole that endures, the remainder that holds more life than the main, the relic more power than the god.

I bear on my body the marks of this faith. Here are the holes drilled into my skull, each set with its gem of consciousness. And the mouths of waste and pleasure. And the scar of my mother.

Who can see with the eye that I see with? Who can hear with the ear I hear with? Who can taste with my tongue, bluntly numb along its right edge? Who can ignore my stench or fragrance as I can? Who can speak my name as I speak it?

We have paid our debt to anonymity under spotlights and guard towers, in the oneness of heaven. We want to return to our different names in the nourishing shadows.

9. God said your name

God said your name today. He said, "Tell me about X." And everybody had a lie you'd like. The solutions for X were all X + 1. X is charming as a firefly, and knows a formula for cold fusion. X's good will is equal to the radius of earth; the fall of the meteorite, the passage of the gritty asteroid, the comet's lonely visit: X notes them all. The biological children of X adore their parent almost as much as the many adopted ones, and all of them are making money close to home. X will donate any duplicate organ for a loved one, and X loves everybody: ask for an eye, a kidney, a lung, a lobe of cerebellum.

And so God, boasting to the devil, said, "Consider my servant X."

10. *I have always thought*

I have always thought the real world was wherever you could die and
know you were dying, even if you had never tasted blood or caught
your newborn by her slippery shoulders, gasping, a streaked plum.

And yet there are two worlds, the unreal and the real. In both the rain
slants and the sun falls. But if a spray of bullets interferes, the difference
is sharper, like a cold snap. And we apologize for living.

Are the President's dreams from the real world? Are there professions
more real than others? Drag queen more than Commerce Secretary?
Computer programmer more than weatherman in Tucson?

In Bangladesh 25 cents a day will save a bamboo stew chef from bond
slavery. Is her life less real now she can control it? When the Ganges
rises, the whole country sinks and clings to its railways. Is Bangladesh
more real underwater?

What are we living for? Isn't it finally to make a rhythm we can live with
daily, that will stress pleasures like bars of melody, strike and hold the

note of our contentment as claims about the real and the unreal pass through it, thick thread through the eye of the whole truth?

Lately I have awakened myself with a sound from my own throat. The place where the knot is loosened becomes a room where I sit, bound by a detachment that grows daily, like a garden snail pulling a hard film over the opening to his shell. Then I am lifted and hurled against a wall, and I mutter.

I thought the world was coming to an end and we would see it. But our eyes will be changed. We will observe like red tail hawks, watching cattle ford neck deep through flooded orchards.

And you ask me if I mean to provide counsel and consolation? Someone else could embody all I am saying in a horse. He would see it through the animal's coffee clear eye, as it stood between traces on cobblestones, pained by a growth above its right fetlock—a soft, gray, carrotlike protrusion. There is a vegetable cart with its meager bounty. There are women leaving houses. The horse looks between smokestacks at the sea, the taint of linseed fumes in its whiskered nostrils, the cold sun hanging in a gray emulsion of cloud cover. The growth on its leg is untended by the horse's owner, the vegetable seller, who is himself covered with moles and wens, a melon-headed, straw-bodied effigy in a great coat and flat cap. The life funneled through the horse's eye is one of motion and rest, pain and less pain, cut by rocking figures of gulls, diluted by rain or a gift pressed up against the lips, in the damp palm of a girl.

Lush, flat land masses, under a thick tent of CO_2, drift toward each other. The sea between becomes a channel, then a river, and one mass slips beneath the other. We might stand on either shore and shake hands. Rain forests upend in the slow, massive collision. Palms lift to elevations where they die. We climb each other. The air thins.

You will hear that death is an entry into the church triumphant, joining the majority, a return to the fathers, a passage into some infinite variety. It may be so. But enjoy the company here.

Three

11. *One wants, the other wants*

One wants, the other wants.

One wants to describe the plots of novels, the other wants to eat dinner. One wants to list the steps for assembly, the other shouts at the racket outside. One wants to pray, the other plans the week's menu. One says just a minute. One says you haven't heard a single thing I've said.

One gives thanks for the accident, for letting things fall as they fall, for life on life's terms. One has a party, one has a funeral. One pets the cat, one puts on a wet bathing suit. One gets the letter bomb, one lives by himself in the woods.

One rages at intellect. One rages at poverty. One rages at the silence of heaven. And there one is in a stocky, young woman with hair down her back, in tight clothes, crossing the street, her chin lifted to defy the traffic. There in a teacher speaking rudely to an eager student, enjoying her little power. There in the men on break, weary at 11 a.m., working beside the English department mansion, their surnames stitched on their uniforms.

One wants to be singled out.

The way a knife will not fully separate a shaft of green onion or stalk of celery it has chopped, that is how one remains attached. The way blinding tears come, mincing yellow onions, that is how knowledge of others blurs. The tedious unpeeling of garlic cloves, especially the finicky thin ones near the heart of the bulb, with purple highlights running through the wrapping and skin, that is how the many inhere, clustered.

But one wants to be singled out, unsheathed from the smother of community, a slim, spiralform, marble word.

That word is your name.

There is in each of us an agent that refuses to die. It makes us, it is driven to form us, and has no idea who we are. Zapped by the ultimate fire blast, it will shift shape and endure. Lodged eventually in a crevice of the dead planet, it will wait millennia for rain.

One loves another, one loves himself. One strides through the color wheel naked with arms outstretched, one crouches drawing diagrams on the bottom of the ocean floor. One worries that his heart is going off, like a week-old carton of milk. One that love is leaking away through some hairfine crack.

And the best things about living—good food and family togetherness, joyful sex, the growing beauty of children, hope for tomorrow—all these will be lost. Any pleasures that might replace them, unthinkable. Returning to God, we will forget whom we loved.

One thinks so. One hopes not.

12. *The numerous, perfumed, small, pale flowers*

The numerous, perfumed, small, pale flowers cluster on bristling, bending stalks. The philosopher tells us they exist for God today. Each flower, 2 to 3.8 centimeters wide, has five sepals, sharp and spear-shaped, five petals, with countless pistils and stamens. He believes there is no time to them. The leaves are divided like feathers into toothed leaflets, 2.5 centimeters long. They are perfect in every moment. That is what he wishes us to know. The thorns are curved and flattened. Their nature is satisfied, they satisfy nature. The plant grows 1.8 to 4.5 meters high, flowering from May through June. It is unashamed to form dense, impenetrable masses, satisfied to take over fields and pastures. We on the other hand, the philosopher assures us, will never be satisfied until we live like that, producing a soul like a small, fleshy, many-seeded fruit.

The gangs, tattooed with each other's names, flourish in the new housing developments. There is no time to them. Vision unites them in inky, bloodstained, impermanent bylaws. They improve their clothing with raucous patches and threads, rips in choice places. Their nature is satisfied, they satisfy nature. Circling us, they achieve an eloquence we hear only in operas. They appear always to be dancing. They are unashamed to form dense, impenetrable masses, satisfied that we are obliged to look within our souls when they make their appearance. The philosopher, glancing from them to us, cannot hide his preference. The sentence he writes to describe our fear is like a prickly, arching stem, drawn quickly through one of our closed palms.

To contradict what he says, I will tell you, you are right to avert your eyes from the corpse on the interstate. To confirm what he says, I will warn you that, great as they are against it happening, the odds are it will happen. And neither the philosopher, who thinks you should live like a flower, nor I, who know you cannot, will tell you what *it* is. You can live without these images. You will be freer without them, just as you would be not knowing the comet will clip North America in your lifetime or that your father collects pornography.

Joy is not the only thing the soul is for. And yet, like the open petals of the newly etched tattoo, you are meant to bring happiness to someone, perhaps even yourself. And you will, from some distance as great or as little as the vine from the root to the rose.

13. If we drive to the meeting with the speakers blasting

If we drive to the meeting with the speakers blasting, needing no one but our addiction, which loves us like a personal God, and if comfort and consolation take us in their body, the clear and glassy corpus that they share, full of laughter and knowing sighs that we can see through, and if suddenly we feel how space starts everywhere, everywhere there is skin, and heads out in all directions, yelling "Glory!"...

Still, at the meeting, the assembly of the lost where we are heading, our heaven will be desert distance, dunes of self-denial. The haunted belly, so subdued, so fluid and contained, knows it, hungering before hunger can begin. And one God, the only God, arcs over all endurance.

And if we dedicate ourselves to happiness and look only on those things that make us happy, and say their names aloud or to ourselves, if we say, "Love," and find we cannot do without the word, that to reject it would make us sweat, lose sleep, and loathe ourselves, what difference is there between saying "Love" or "God" (a word we also need) and our addiction?

15. We have reached a place where nothing looks back

We have reached a place where nothing looks back except what we know. Those who greet us raise a hand, step back one foot at a time, reflecting our gestures. Nothing looks back from rock face or tree trunk except our words—*face, trunk*.

I whisper this.

A student wrote from North Africa, in the desert he understood why there was only one God. Here I know why there are many.

that may contain a violin or high-powered rifle. In this one a collection of objects—an answering machine, a camera, a pair of binoculars, a laptop computer. In another, moving service, a .38 caliber revolver. In every period of worship these things take on the numinosity of faith, each with its inherent worth abruptly revealed.

Theologians spring up among our friends. Our visitor, they say, had been watching us, studying us, there was some plan. We join them in speculating on the location of our possessions, the new plane they occupy, and their miraculous return.

The man spraying to check for fingerprints says this scrotebag will not be back. He finds nothing and crowns each empty place with a halo of soot. His severity and solemnity are like John Knox's, if Knox lit up after church and complained bitterly about sin moving into the better neighborhoods, because of the mayor's new policies. Knox fuming, after his fulminations in the pulpit. Knox driving off in a crime-scene van.

We attached ourselves to things, and now we feel like amputees. The wrist of the watch, severed. The fingers snapped from the neck of the violin. The eye of the camcorder plucked out. Where the laptop sat, a lapse.

We try to feel lucky in our violation. He could have burned down the house. He could have kidnapped the children. We could have surprised him and driven after him and been shot dead through the windshield. He didn't take the wedding album. He didn't take the TV. Here, safe in its drawer, he didn't take this. There, in plain sight on the desk, he didn't take that.

Now anyone we pass is a felon or an upstanding citizen. We listen to the gospel of electronic security. Listen and believe. But it is not a religion that brings joy or consolation. We enter the feast days of anxiety, the high holidays of suspicion.

This letter goes out with a list of things encoded that we still possess.

Four

16. *All my concern*

All my concern is for what you will not give away, what you keep to yourself, withheld in your soul's shut and crowded closet. You have something in there, don't you?

If I appeared to you in dreams, either as myself, a capsule of ink, or something else, a pileated woodpecker or thick dust, you know you would wonder about it all day long. I want to know what I mean to you.

You would like to press your thumb into the sun's clay and the moon's plaster, you would like your voice to activate the summer night, you would like to harrow hell. I'm not saying you can't. But you need a good reason.

Compare the blueprint of the skull with the topology of heaven. God has a wonderful plan for your life. But which is it?

Consider the child who left a nickel on her brother's grave. She gave something she cared about, not everything she had.

Given earth, air, water, fire, we return steel, steam, saliva, salt. Given flesh, we return waste. Given love ... But let's be fair to ourselves. Given love, we return earth, air, water, fire, flesh.

But not everything, right? And even if we could give everything, our all, our entire reserve, the gross domestic product of the dream life and the net profit of our cells, something would be kept back, which we don't know how to give or give up. Money we forgot we buried. The squirrel hiding on the other side of the tree trunk.

If you could think of me as that part you cannot part with, no matter how hard you try, then the surface tension of the word, the skin of sound and form, would split like a beetle's wing casings and the secret take flight into the known.

We imagine perfection as an equal balance of trade, recycling, ZPG, a world at peace, coming together yet staying alone, *mens sana in corpore sano*, an ox allowed to graze as it treads the grain. But if God were to give you another of his unspeakable gifts, wouldn't you scream?

Take off the onion skin of everyday life. Remove the rind of the social being. Peel away the barbed leaves of language that protect the dumb

heart. Chop through the woody shell and crack the nut of privacy.
Hand it over, a pale green shoot like the germ of a garlic clove—
yourself.

I will accept anything you offer with a nod and a smile. And as you offer
a fingernail and say is this enough, as you offer a tooth and say is this
enough, as you offer half your genetic material in the pith of an egg or
the head of a spermatozoon and say is this enough, as you offer a lung, a
kidney, bone marrow, blood, and say is this enough, I will smile and nod
and say, "Do you think it's enough?"

We live in the hollow of an immense desire.

Life ends with a bonus, the means to our death. We are added to zero,
then multiplied by it.

Weeping, wailing, gnashing of teeth, but it will be as if you left the
world propped to take the sun against a stucco wall, between a patch of
thistles and a heat pump, your last pint of fortified wine warming
between your thighs. That is to say, for all its effect on you, the
lamentation of survivors will be no more than a starling's monologue in
the parking lot adjacent. The unendurable roar of storm on the sun's

surface is more audible. You will not even hear yourself. And yet your absence will leave a void like the extinction of the cornflower.

Now is the only acceptable time. But there is also later, in a moment or two, just a second, in a minute, tomorrow or the day after, any day, first thing in the morning, in the late afternoon, after dinner and before bed. If you can pray the way Scheherazade spun tales, you will pass hardly missing a beat.

You can't take it with you. Why not leave it with me?

19. Eternity

Eternity will be strange at first, because there will be no *at first*.

Still, try this. Think of blank times with other people's habits, when you had to eat with strangers and strange hosts, and follow their customs and rituals at table. A glassy patience took over. Through its panels even watching was a kind of starvation, a sort of drought. The portions lay stranded on large plates. The grace was minimal but stiflingly pious. There was nothing to drink. And the time ahead filled a football stadium.

Then you discovered their peculiar passions—genre fiction, dog racing. Suddenly you were an umbrella stand of questions. Time, almost like the drink you were denied, turned almost sexy. When you left, sated with information, and even a little drunk with a fizzy affection for the plain, stolid family of doorstops, they invited you back.

Heaven may turn out to be one long church service, with everyone in the choir. Or Thanksgiving dinner. You will be one in a crowd, singing Handel. Or stranded forever, eating with your extended family. If what they say is true, you'll be happy just to be there in your seat behind the pillar, near the back. Or at the children's table, in the corner.

Her mother was drying her hair. She'd been sick for two days and was taking medication. I was downstairs, reading, when my wife called and said our daughter had fainted. Our child, in her nightgown, her thick short hair now dry, was sitting on the floor before the sink in the bathroom. Her face was like putty, her pink lips gray, she wasn't wearing her glasses. Her mother remained cool, speaking to her, calling her name. She turned in my direction, and there was such a look of departure in her eyes, I wondered if we'd get her back. Her: our child. In a soft voice she said she couldn't see. She was like a traveler who'd gone to live in another country and stopped writing home. Then she regained her sight, her color returned. Soon she was chattering about how frightened she'd been, but also about what she'd done all day at home in bed—reading, homework, crosswords. The light had become too bright for her, she said, and she felt she couldn't speak, except softly. That was all. The first time she was sick, when she was a little thing, she had become dumb, an empty puppet. We had seen that face again—of a creature who had no earthly idea what had happened. She looked at us, her mother and father, as if we did not exist and as if we were the ones who had done this to her.

And that is how they look at us, both the damned and the saved. That is how they regard the living. And yet we can try to soften the picture. Look at your own hand and try to believe that once this thing grasped the heart of the sun. Look at it and imagine it returning to that heart, thrust there. And you follow it, pulled by the wrist, your body a banner of streaming atoms, signed with an unrecognizable name, which nevertheless is you.

The living will always misinterpret the last look we give them. It does not mean they are nothing. And it does not mean they are guilty. It means they are coming too.

20. Out of the whirlwind

Out of the whirlwind's barrel-chested, charcoal body, crossing streets,
sparkling with ignited transformers that flashed like cameras: one death.
The city half-conscious under its upturned trees, its crushed roofs,
knotted powerlines: one death. Oak, hackberry, magnolia, hickory sucked
out of their sockets in the earth, by the thousands. Blue jays, robins,
cardinals, grackles confused, crossing among crossed, confused wires.

One death among the deaths. One loss among the losses.

Reek of cracked cedar and pine. Fragrance of freshly sawn wood, green
wood, heartwood, damp with life, scattered, chopped and stacked for
the fire and the chipper. Tree bases upended like manhole covers to the
underworld, root faces like propellers of sunken ships. Leaves, for which
there is no formula to produce an accurate count, withering in
premature autumn. The urban forest sacked and looted.

And churches knocked down ecumenically. And homes leveled
according to the most random plan. And schools. And stores.

One loss. One death.

William Blake said the devil made nature. He scoffed at Wordsworth
who loved it. Wordsworth who loved scenery. Blake who loved the body
of God. Let Wordsworth praise the action whereby lightning changes
polarity and the vacuum between heaven and earth establishes its roving
temple of destruction. Design without intent is not evil, even as it flays a
mobile home park. Blake was wrong, but right to scoff.

Inside the phenomenon we face—who knows? It is traveling there that
makes our tongues cleave to the roof of our mouths. And it seems we
have been ruined, forced out on the street, given the stark news that our
enemies are right to hate us. The approach emulsifies hope. The
horizon eats our names.

And what of it? Windows rattle, the car veers off the road and rolls.
We're lucky to be awake as the jaws of life shear through metal.

Inside the phenomenon, every roof in the neighborhood explodes like a
bad theory. And the ancient red oak falls toward the picnickers under
the band shell. Soon one of them will enter the event alone. One will go

inside, where it is hard to get a message in or out. We will ask him many questions when he returns, but he will never return completely. In the hospital, the sloping bed where he lies will tilt him slowly back, then tip him over out of reach.

Meanwhile look at him, in there, under the fallen tree, inside the phenomenon. A singularity, a unity, a oneness that is not atonement. No other way to count, outside the event horizon, watching the phenomenon recede. One death among the deaths. One loss among the losses.

This morning on the way to work I was stuck behind a kind of vehicle I did not recognize. For a mile I studied what looked like a massive beak, painted orange, or one of those folded fortune-telling papers that have four points and cover the hand, but in this case enormous and made of steel. Earth clung to its lips. Or were they seams? When I had decided it was a colossal posthole digger, I was able to pass the truck that pulled it. Then I saw the slender bole and trembling leaves of the Bradford pear tree nested in the huge cradle. And the logo of a tree replacement service. The machine would plunge the living sapling into earth where some older tree had been ripped out. I thought of Blake etching the scene on a copper plate. Of Wordsworth admiring the occupation—ten thousand of these plantings at a glance.

We lived complacently—forgive us—among green hills far away. One death has changed us all. One loss. It is right to count this way.

Five

21. History

History is not as porous to God as I thought and the gaps grow farther apart.

We can be like the child whose sister was raped and murdered who said at the funeral, "All the happy times I spent with you and will spend with you, I enjoyed and will enjoy." Or like the woman who has one memory of the mother who died when she was eight. Shouting at her in front of a closet.

In the meantime, put in the eyes of wish fulfillment, put out the hand with its five hungers, put on the skin of fiction.

When, with the help of micromachines, I am able to alter my shape at will, indeed to give myself a lifeshape without a death instinct, when I have conquered death in this body or another substitute body, while retaining enough of my soul to enjoy it, will I be worrying you or myself about what God wishes for his children?

This, as they say, lies years in the future. And if we are made or remade from remnants, thawed and brought back, it is years in the future. Burn your body and you will be safe, probably. Or maybe not. We are graverobbers—the museums, the traveling exhibits.

Eternal life may be coming back to this world perfected, without your permission.

The creation of diamonds. A blip. The crocheting of DNA. A blip. Cross-stitch of the bilateral face. A blip. Condensation of tears from Paleozoic seas. A blip. Endurance of the strange, the doubly strange, the triply strange particle. A blip. The time it takes to bring you past the kiss, past the coupling, past the nearly dispassionate concentration, so that time can stop. Blip. Blip. Blip.

But the nine months, the terrible twos, the childhood, adolescence, adulthood, all the elongation of growing up and its estranging inwardness, the longed for reconciliation of parent and child before death, the wait for rebirth: these take forever.

What are you thinking now about eternal life? That it will be life eternally. And the bloody news at breakfast will continue. And the free

64

floating anxiety will continue. And the cosmic indifference will continue. But so will nakedness with my wife, black coffee in the morning, being read Dickens by my daughter before bedtime.

What are you thinking now about eternal life? That I will shed my guilt like sodden running clothes and hear the hymn of praise beginning in my throat as the multifoliate radiance anoints my face like a stiff hot shower and blurs every memory of earth.

What are you thinking now about eternal life? That I will wake up, stare at the twilit room, move over to mold my body to Amy's, my left hand on her right breast, and go back to sleep for half an hour.

When the preacher stood before the class that day in June, 1968, and said that history was a river that God entered at will, he wished to console us for the assassinations. To comfort those who mourned. But no one seemed to understand. Perhaps no one was mourning.

Perhaps he should have said that history was a freeway that God entered at will. Perhaps he should have said that history was a TV show that God interrupted at will. Perhaps he should have said that history was six periods of stone boredom five consecutive days a week and an

afterschool job and a weekend of chores that God canceled at will.
He said history was a river. And the only river we knew was the Los
Angeles, a concrete flood channel we had never seen in flood, running
alongside the freeway like a giant gutter.

And the killing that spring had occurred on people's 16th birthdays.

Behind, beyond, before and after, existing now but separately, accessible
in some special instances, like prayer, but present only as a listening,
present only as a signal coming from a distance, present only as a
silence.

We can live eternally like that. But for the time being, we will live as we
are, for as long as we can.

These are the gifts of the spirit. The belief that the body is enough. The
belief that love is a god. The belief that the next world is this world
perfected.

22. As the couple turn toward each other

As the couple turn toward each other in the dark, without speaking; as the impulse to kiss the man or woman beside you is restrained; as a voice on the telephone slowly brings a face to mind; so prayer commences, strangely intimate with everything it thinks of.

Ed Bryant has rejected his new kidney. Sally Rogers, a friend of Missy Edwards, begins chemotherapy this week. Robert Powers, our janitor, is resting comfortably at home. The Niederthals and their children are still waiting permission to leave Tunisia. Hal Anderson is stuck on the tarmac in Detroit. Longtime executive director of the Sunday School Board, Erlise Hopson, was found in the bathroom of her apartment at the Millicent Christian Retirement Center. Let us also remember the Kurdish separatists in Turkey and Iraq.

Prayer aligns us with random forces. It is an impulse among impulses. It is like shining a flashlight into the night sky in your backyard. The light from prayer diverges, so its intensity (the flux per unit area) grows weaker the farther it goes. Mainly prayer is scattered (dispersed in new directions, if you like) by other prayers. In urban settings, there are lots of them in the atmosphere, and they deflect each other toward different ends. And yet our prayer heads into space, full of presumption that the speed of light will carry it beyond the Pleiades.

He sweated blood. He knew he was going to die. He prayed. He sweated, not blood but drops like blood. Arterial. Pulsing. As if to sweat this way might kill him. He could see how he would die and asked not to die. The one to whom he prayed answered with silence. Clasped by a hand of silence, at the end of an arm of silence, it was a cup of silence, holding the countless counted beads of his unanswered answered prayer.

So your face burns when you say, "I'll pray for you." So you believe a signal bounces off eternity and strikes the object of your prayer, and you blush to believe it, that is, to say so in so many words.

For it is as if in the presence of one we worked with daily and respected, with whom we spoke in familiar yet businesslike tones about matters of concern—writing reports, making proposals—a scene as formalized as liturgy presented us to one another naked. Or it is as if in the presence of one we loved, who would willingly undress for us, we pictured another life, in another place, with someone else.

I understand your reaction. *My* face burns.

I'll pray for you. I'll eat for you. I'll drink for you. I'll speak for you. I'll breathe for you. I'll write for you. I'll call for you. I'll work for you. I'll sing for you. I'll play for you. I'll live for you. I'll die for you. I'll change for you. I will speak to the nonexistent about your existence. I will add my impotence to your impotence.

And yet if everything prayed one prayer, it would have to be heard, wouldn't it? Perhaps that prayer is *Let me be*. That prayer is heard.

23. Easier to think about the body

Easier to think about the body of the comet than the human body. Easier to see its white hair stretch out in the solar wind than to visualize a synapse in the brain. And to understand the progress through bleak space, thousands of years to complete an orbit—that is easier than to picture a life.

And yet if I told you that death would set you in the heavens like a comet, how would you live your life, knowing your state of grace would be to form a head of ice, hurled beyond Pluto, rapt in a meditation of the sun?

Your hip aches. Your rectum itches. Your hair falls out or is replaced by coarse white wire. Your nostrils and ears fill with bristles (these also white). The skin around your eyes crumples into wizened crepe and droopy sacking. And your brain empties its rooms. You wander through vacancies.

I write to you today about soteriology. But first, let me tell you about the spring. Inside its dykes the city is on fire with dogwood blossoms, denser and whiter than cataracts. The comet has dragged its whiteness through the trees and it hurts the eyes. Knowing it can't last hurts, too.

The world sees the lonely traveler and calls, "Comrade!" Surely the comet has a soul. Surely, in some age we can easily imagine (more easily than infancy), the doctrine of salvation fell from its wake and caressed the planet and created rain.

Thus every eye that looks back at us seems to speak a word. Thus every surface that surprises us with touch seems to know us.

I am talking to the least of you. That man squatting fully alert behind his desk. That boy between two desperate parents, slapping himself on the chin. That girl just before she understands the powerlessness of beauty. That woman hiding inside her house. Those fishing with their own flesh for bait. Those too hungry to lift food to their mouths. Those posing naked. Those with them.

We fly off. We rush headlong, growing harder and colder. We leave a star behind and find a star before us. It becomes a face, its mouth uttering love and its breath flaying us alive. We rush off. We fly headlong.

And all the while, throughout our lives, our solitude defines us like a body we wear inside our body, bone in muscle, muscle under skin, thought inside of skull, light within the eyes, until we think salvation, if

it comes, will come to save that solitude.

24. If God were not promiscuous

If God were not promiscuous, we would have no one to blame for our loneliness, no one to forgive.

Listening to the story of his betrayals is like hearing about the social life of a small town we've broken down in, while waiting for a part to arrive. In the course of two or three hot afternoons, it is possible to become intimate with details so uninteresting the earth seems to freeze beneath the zodiac.

To be truthful, the objects of God's love are more numerous than we can ever hope to accept. Clasped and breathing together, it is not clear that the name he calls is ours, despite his assurances.

It is at such times, faced with the enormity of God's license, that we turn childish and require some gift as compensation for his philandering. A weight beside us, as we lie in bed. A shape beside us, like a spouse or a dog, a long-boned hound, to make up for his absence.

It is pointless to accuse and make him suffer, plot against and think of destroying him. To bring God down, while locked in love with someone else, some galaxy cruising the outskirts of his thighs, would provide a taste of ashes.

There is nothing to be done but to enjoy vicariously the fact that, at every moment, God is with a lover, throwing his head back, wailing like a woman giving birth.

25. Forgive me, Lord

Recently I learned that God no longer delighted in my existence. He

had grown homesick for the child I was, and regarded the balding,

graying, overweight, five-nine middleaged man with some

disenchantment. His heart did not dance to see me dress myself, his

bowels turned cold as I drank my morning coffee. I heard that,

contented as I was with myself—my daily habits of work, exercise,

leisure, and sleep—he believed I should be dissatisfied, as he was.

Despite the years it had taken for me to become myself—the scarred

face I shaved without cutting—he wished I had become someone else,

or had never become, had stayed the plump, unselfconscious boy of

three, standing between his father's crouching legs, encircled by arms

on the front lawn beside the sprinkler head, snapped in black and white,

in a glow of summer. I understood the words repeated to me, but found

it hard to choke down the question: "Who needs him?" He must have

heard the prayer I made to the windstorm that sheared oaks one block

over. He must have seen me refuse to answer the phone when Mother

called. Read what I wrote about his favorite poet, the one who copied

verses verbatim from the Bible. Tasted the bile in my throat, when one

he adored spoke my name. Singed his fingertips on the dry ice where I stored my grudges, riffling through them, looking for the one that carried his name. So his message came, and I laid it up in my heart. Which of us now is obliged to forgive?

Now I am brooding over abstract states. It is that time of year the onion grass sprouts among yellow winter blades, the remaining oak leaves stir about, the exposed earth at the base of the trees shows damply. A fresh gust raises dead leaves randomly, by one corner, to make sure they are dead, or like bandages, checking for violets, and drops them down again, hinged on a crisp edge. And yet, one leaf will lose its grip and go tumbling, and others around seem to look after it.

It is nearing the time when one said to the dogwood where he was nailed, "I know you pity me. Never again will you grow like the oak and provide lumber for crucifixions. You will be slender, and your blossoms, two long and two short petals, will form a cross. At the tip of each petal, a wound where the nail bit, rusty with blood. At the heart of each flower, a crown of thorns. In this transformation, remembering me, you will be forgiven."

A curse alters only the one who utters it. But something passes between the forgiver and the forgiven that changes them both. One opens the injured eyelid and sees the wound has healed. And the other feels lighter, as when the pod unlocks and the plumed seed learns it flies.

76

Six

26. In the Clouds

Simply by thinking I stood among the clouds. They surrounded and passed me, being and becoming. Blood released into clear water. Breath into cold air. Formlessness entering form, forced into form. Breathing felt huge then smaller than a cell. And I thought, "Don't the clouds themselves feel ambivalent between heaven and earth, hardly more substantial than their shadows? They come into being as randomly as we do. And they disintegrate. They go. What is the lifespan of a cloud? We want to float among them, loving the colossal, shot through with crooked pins of fire, towering side by side."

How did I get up there? I was thinking about changing my life and wanted to talk to a cloud, since clouds are always changing. And the clouds said, "How long has it been since you felt completely happy? Because you are always dissatisfied, always disappointed—it has been a long time. Talk to us. We are admired and disparaged. We are less than everything you compare us to except nothingness. We are not nothing. Talk to us. Our silence, like the new shapes we are forever assuming, will be sympathetic. In the clouds, you will understand yearning as you never have and come back to earth changed, who knows how?

Surrender your skin, your bones. But we will not hold you up. We are as ineffectual as cattle, turning steep white faces beside the road, to watch you spin out of control. Placid as the love of God. Fall out of the sky, go sliding down the icy face of the air, we will watch, a little lightning might flicker in a distant bulb of fiber glass. Come to us as the exhalation of your speech, the spirit trapped inside your webs of flesh torn free. We are the embodiment of detachment. You know us best when we are most distant and you are least afraid, when we are most moving and you are unmoved."

Brothers and sisters, consider the taste of cloud in a Sherpa's mouth, of fog in a surfer's throat. Consider the flocculent muscle of the cumulus. The icy elevation of the cirrus. But especially the thunderhead, full of zeal, hurrying in with its beveled wind, white slanting rain, its electric personality, its aftermath. Consider how the clouds predict one another and how they break up, pulling a new body behind them. The farmer's wide open perspective. The office worker's sidelong glimpse. Weeks of drab overcast. A single afternoon of separate sailwhite drifters. Clouds flat and dull as lampblack, clouds with the contours of the brain, clouds like sheets of paper. I have read that even in an empty sky there exists water vapor enough to make a cloud. Belief enough to make a God.

As they change, clouds grow neither better nor worse. They alter because it is their nature to alter. They can fill us with joy or cast a stagnant sorrow over our days. Such is life under the clouds. In the clouds it is different. But if we live in the clouds, we have to take the earth with us.

27. For the Birds

When you wake up, raising the film over your eyes, in a hollow of boughs or bark, you are always hungry. And you all talk at once. Each twig has an opinion and holds a singing fabric sewn with discussions of lice, offspring, height above ground, eyesight, mates, one-night stands, best routes to Canada once the warm weather comes, the taste of this bug, that bug, spittle needed to mat human hair, mud's pliancy, the housework of the sky. We think that none of you has an insight into the afterlife. But you all remember birth and the cramped translucent dark before the break-out.

I am bored. I need birds. Not flight but activity, not serene detachment sailing but intense engagement hunting. Look me in the eyes, frontal, head on. And I admire you. Study me askance. And I adore you. Even the moa in the museum case. The trinket hanging from the Christmas tree.

Incurious witnesses, feathers dabbled in blood, poking your noses in the wounded hands and feet. What did St. Francis tell you? Be yourselves, little ones, and you will praise God.

For how many of us were you the first word?

Trouble sleeping, I think of you in the netted aviary. There among reaching fronds and dangling flowers, you hovered at my sister's washed floating hair, patient to take a single sand-colored strand which, buoyed by static, reached out half-limp to be taken. She felt it go with a little cry when the root broke from its anchor of scalp-skin.

And this morning, there's an oil smear on the sliding glass door to the patio, and in it, dangling gray breast feathers—five of them, like milkweed fluff. One of you caromed off the hard sky and left this pattern, as precise as fish scales, scalloped on the glass like a record in rock. Veronica's napkin. The Shroud of Turin.

Woodpeckers, hairy or downy. Red bellied. Pileated. Flickers. Cardinals. Brown thrashers. A single rosebreasted grosbeak. Once, a tumbling flock of drunken cedar waxwings, chirping like crickets. Red tail hawks with breasts like lampshades. Great horned owls conversing at dawn, in January. Screech owls in their red phases. Mockingbirds copying mockingbirds. Chimney swifts back from Peru to the same elementary school chimney. Kingbirds on powerlines. Blue birds in pairs. Blue jays in gangs. To be a man who surrounds his house with birds. To be a woman visited by wings. To say to the turkey vulture overhead, "Sister." To say, "Brother," to the starling in the swirling flock.

If your call and response first thing in the morning make us hold hands and smile in the dark, as we lie in bed, it's because we're not alone in the world. And when letters like this one are written, it is because we are.

28. To the Trees

How do you feel as you rear up or hunch over to seek sunlight? When young, as pliant almost as water, when old, second only to rock. I think you must feel that roots are better than roads, that the avenue to the sky is best straight up or crookedly up. That whatever happens around you is no more than rain or snow, even the building that embraces you, even the saw and stump remover that eat up all trace of you.

For the present you are stone, but let the wind rise and you sing and dance like bamboo. Your children are the dapples of sunshine in shade. Your ancestors bask on the mossy facets of your bark. And within is a coming and going of thirst and records of thirst, of flesh that fire would love to taste. You know the math that sends the fire branching upwards. You know the myth that lights the candelabra. Planets and stars gleam on your smallest twig ends.

You have held back the body of the wind. You have held back the onslaught of the heat. You have given me the idea of depth. You have revealed the nesting of microcosms, all while staying in one place. We came down from you and stood upright like you. Because you will not rush along with us we cut you down.

It's what's inside and outside that counts. Hollow with ant meal, your blossoms and leaves still come. Solid as granite, you can stand deadgray for decades. You bleed, you break, you rot. The massive inner framework fades, and there's a limp limb, a branch of brown leaves among green, a bridge across a stream, a back-breaking fall on a ranch-style house. You rot, you break, you bleed. You go up in smoke, sideways in fire, down and down and down.

In my metamorphosis, she appears in the doorway, wet from the shower and looking for a towel. We catch each other by surprise, goddess and little boy, and we are both changed. At times she is a row of eucalyptus, where the trees and the sunlight between them are the same smooth color. It is my fate to hunt for her everywhere except where that tree grows. At times I am pyracantha under her windowsill, burning to speak. It is her fate to believe I have nothing to say.

You are life to those who hold fast to you, but standing apart on the lawn, don't you all long for the forest canopy? To join and blot out the sky, with a dancing floor lifted to the sun for hawks and monkeys and orchids in the higher parts of shadow? Don't you all long to rise up and erect your shade?

Let me be neither branch nor leaf but one facet of your bark, deeply incised on all sides, gray in dry sunny weather, and in rain, showing a face of turquoise.

29. On the Street

He jogs in, a v of sweat on his t-shirt. He strides in, pushing a baby
carriage. Wearing a Walkman, he saunters in. He barrels in in his truck,
and stops, and gets out. He tells the taxi driver to let him off here. He
thanks the person who gave him a lift, opens the car door, and invites
her to stay. Brakes his bicycle at the brush heap in the cul de sac,
dismounts, and starts calling our names. Our first names. Appears one
day, like the blossoms on the redbud, and captures our attention. We
know it's spring, and we know him.

What's the word on the street? The word is made flesh on the street.
The word is made person, place, and thing. The word is steel, concrete,
fiber-optic cable, ceramic and saliva, aluminum and blood, axle grease
and fingernails, hair and glass. It is the leaf of the sidewalk weed and
the soft desiring soul inside the truck cab. It is the footprint tracked a
little ways beyond the puddle and the foot still thinking of where it
stepped. Anonymous and public, the word is that if you're good, you'll
be happy, if you're happy, you'll be good. Suffer and remain private.
Receive aid, and see your savior on the news. Out the door, into the
blaring, shining welcome, from which there is no escape, the word on

the street is lord. Tang of diesel fumes, fellow fragrance of men and women, music of the spheres of influence burning to illuminate the word, the word in every molecule that starts a sense, these—and that face that passes and travels with you a little way beyond the sight of it. They are the word on the street. And the word is knowledge like a cellphone ringing with all the others.

Inside, behind the showroom window, two men in shirtsleeves and ties and a woman in her power suit watched. One held a telephone. Outside we passed the group beginning to assemble around the lady who lay on her right cheek. She wore a felt hat and a cloth coat, both a grayer version of her blue eye, her left eye which stared at our feet. The right side of her face—cheek, eye, half her mouth—was pressed hard against the sidewalk. The half of her mouth we could see showed, in its grin, an effort to do or say—no one knew. Her eye, watching our feet, was painted marble, showing outer and inner knowledge, straining to know more. As if she were studying the street itself—the pavement where we were passing and our feet—studying for a clue to why she had fallen there, why she walked there, lived there, put on her old lady's attire on an early spring day, and went out, to do errands, and found her way to this vigil, this post.

What was she looking at? At the grain of the cement she felt under her cheek and its color. At the rims of shoe soles that stopped and those that pivoted and moved on. The soles made a grainy scraping that her hidden ear caught and she was looking at the source of that sound. There is too much on the street. All you can do is know the smallest portion. May it save her.

30. Through the Waves

If I spoke to you through the waves, which one would catch your attention, the ripple that wet your knee or the beach-pounder shaking your bed? If I spoke to you through the waves, would you remember what I said as a series of glittering, nostalgic video images, far from the ocean, each as harmless as cotton floss?

Small, gray, glassy, like a pleasant hour reading, transparent to its heart of jellyfish and seaweed. Large, swift, green, opaque and grinning whitely, asking for a quick response. Unanswerable, coming down startled, all bulk and foam, which you must dive under. Each bearing a message. Lovely swelling blue, giving you time to move into position, just as it peaks and you feel its force behind you. Black, making her arms glisten as she swims at night, belly and face like candles of phosphorus. Colorless, dismal rippling, coming to shore over shingle, cold enough to turn fingernails purple. And the warm giant that beckons before it sweeps you under to toil among churning roots.

If I spoke to you through the waves, would you see your face reflected in the upthrust wall of words? If I spoke to you through the waves, would your revery before their arrival ever turn into understanding?

To quiet myself I used to remember being lifted and carried by them, buoyed as they broke around me, and standing up in the shallows among the frothy rubble of their collapse, then wading back out, swimming out to meet them as they continued coming to shore. That would help me to fall asleep when I first began to live apart from them. As years passed, and I moved deeper inland, I would dream of them. In one recurring dream I walked along a sea wall and they broke against it, and I saw in their explosions, they were made of pigeon feathers or anthracite or my parents' faces or red oak leaves. Though enormous they broke slowly and benignly, their spray drifting like confetti and dissolving in air. But once I began to dream of them I no longer tried to remember them when I couldn't sleep: to do so only made me more wakeful. A time came when I no longer dreamt of them and they ceased altogether to have any reality for me. They had been lifted and shaped by homesickness. They had emerged composed of dreamstuff for reasons I could never fathom. Now they are a single idea: the image of body and soul together as one.

If I spoke to you through the waves, would you see that I mean more than the moon and less, more than the wind and less, more than the sea floor and less, more than more, less than less? If I spoke to you through the waves, how many times would I have to repeat myself?

Out of chaos, beyond theory, into a life that peaks and breaks, the wave emerges. The shore where it dies lies ahead and waits, unseen. A life must peak as it rides up the shallow approach, steepen, and break. I want you to think of yourself like that, of your body and soul like that, one flesh traveling to shore, to collapse, all that way to end by darkening the sand and evaporating. Where do you go? You repeat in other waves, repeat and repeat. Each bears a message. Each has a meaning.

If I spoke to you through the waves, I would continue to bring them to life until, looking at how they laid themselves at your feet, at how even the greatest ended as film on sand, you said, "Someone is trying to tell me something." And I would not stop.

The Author

Mark Jarman was born in Mount Sterling, Kentucky, and grew up in California and Scotland. He is Centennial Professor of English at Vanderbilt University in Nashville, Tennessee. He is the author of eight books of poetry: *North Sea* (1978), *The Rote Walker* (1981), *Far and Away* (1985), *The Black Riviera* (1990), *Iris* (1992), *Questions for Ecclesiastes* (1997), *Unholy Sonnets* (2000), and *To the Green Man* (2004). Jarman's awards include a Joseph Henry Jackson Award for his poetry in 1974, three NEA grants in poetry in 1977, 1983, and 1992, and a fellowship in poetry from the John Simon Guggenheim Memorial Foundation for 1991–1992. His book *The Black Riviera* won the 1991 Poets' Prize. *Questions for Ecclesiastes* was a finalist for the 1997 National Book Critics Circle Award in poetry and won the 1998 Lenore Marshall Poetry Prize from the Academy of American Poets and *The Nation* magazine.

17. Life is an end

How urgently we try to put birth behind us, the union of microbes, that crude mechanism, to get away from its obsessive drive, to get away from the murky gestation chamber with its waxy blinders and coiled tubes, to be done with it, to get out any way we can or die trying.

And when we do escape, life pursues us. Or, rather, the place we have escaped from comes after us. We look back and see the things we desire, which we thought lay ahead of us, calling us from behind. Home. Success and sex. Peace. All of them call. And we end up where we started, unable to tell why we ever wished to escape.

Then, death begins. A night like one we have known but forgotten recommences. The moving edifice of eternity, sent on its way, is sleek as a doublewide, towed at 70 mph down the interstate. Eyes that saw us last try to peer beyond the horizon. A little gossip swirls like candy wrappers in our wake.

Where are we going? There's a shady lakeside spot where the swans glide and hiss. There's a hot heart in a compost heap. There's another planet. There's plenty of room to spare outside the wobbling bubble of time and space.

Death is abstract? Life is concrete?

Now life is abstract, drawing away from birth, from the nothing before conception, always pulling out of the station and heading off somewhere the others can't see. Mother is left behind with her body. Father with his advice. Brothers and sisters, removed to different cities. One forwarding address follows another. Life enters memory faster every day.

And death is concrete, a growing together, a meeting of parallel lines, a fusion of joints, a distinct massing of days, the body accepting its final illness, the vanishing point like a mustard seed sprouting the multiple and enormous branches of pollen-gold, flowering oblivion.

Keep thinking this way and you may console yourself endlessly.

18. *Despite the ash in the air*

Despite the ash in the air, the smoldering underbrush up to the edge of the highway, the lifeguards working the beach in cotton surgical masks, it's not the end of the world.

Despite the child building his pipe bomb, the parents in their startled postures, lying in different parts of the house, the animals waiting their turn, it's not the end of the world.

Despite the exile from your neighborhood, the place you have found to sleep, rolled in wet sheets of plastic, it's not the end of the world.

Despite the Valley of Kings submerged, the pristine Moon polluted, the sky a junkyard of orbiting debris, it's not the end of the world.

Despite the lesion that dims the eyesight and the tremor that stills with the day's first drink, it's not the end of the world.

New houses are going up along the fault line, orderlies make a ruckus round the clock in the corridor, we eat and sleep, though no longer together.

So, what is the end of the world?

The eyesight smudged. The pipe bomb taped to the animal. Ash filling the air and the Valley of Kings. The lifeguards afraid for their lives.